Marcie Meier

D1603772

THE WONDER OF BECOMING YOU

How a Jewish Girl Grows Up

DR. MIRIAM GROSSMAN

THE WONDER
OF
BECOMING YOU

HOW A JEWISH GIRL GROWS UP

FELDHEIM PUBLISHERS

Jerusalem / New York

First published in 1988

Copyright © 1988 by Dr. Miriam Grossman

Philipp Feldheim Inc.
200 Airport Executive Park, Spring Valley, NY 10977

Feldheim Publishers Ltd.
POB 35002/Jerusalem, Israel

Library of Congress Cataloging-in-Publication Data

Grossman, Miriam.
The wonder of becoming you.

ISBN 0-87306-438-0

Summary: An explanation for adolescent girls of the changes that take
place at puberty and how Jewish tradition views this and other related
aspects of becoming a woman.

1. Jewish girls — Conduct of life — Juvenile literature.
2. Modesty — Religious aspects — Judaism — Juvenile literature.
3. Puberty — Juvenile literature.
[1. Adolescent girls — Conduct of life. 2. Jewish religious education. 3.
Puberty] I. Title.
BM727.G76 1988   296.7'4'088055   88-7093

10 9 8 7 6

Printed in Israel

To my parents

A glossary of Hebrew and Yiddish words
appears at the end of this book.

ב״ה

I have carefully gone through Dr. Grossman's book about how a Jewish girl grows up.

It is written with delicacy and in sensitive consonance with Torah teachings and values.

May Hashem grant the author great hatzlacha in her undertaking to guide young bnos Yisrael to know themselves as vessels for avodas Hashem.

Sincerely,

Yaakov Weinberg

Dear Parent,

Each year, myriad books are published all over the world. Although thousands are books of Jewish interest, and hundreds concern Torah-related topics, very few succeed in dealing with difficult, contemporary issues in a simple, clear, and fully Torah-oriented manner. If one is fortunate enough to find a book which does, and if, in addition to its other qualities, it not only explains, but inspires, then one has found a treasure indeed. We at Feldheim consider *The Wonder of Becoming You – How a Jewish Girl Grows Up* by Dr. Miriam Grossman to be one of those rare treasures.

On the advice of a well-known *gadol*, the *rav* of a girls' yeshiva sought an Orthodox, female doctor to speak to his pre-teen students about the physiological changes which they were, or would shortly be, experiencing. Dr. Miriam Grossman was contacted and she agreed to lecture on this topic, which soon branched out to include not only the obvious physical changes, but the spiritual development which should accompany them. The lectures were so successful that Dr. Grossman was persuaded to use them as the basis for a book, thereby enabling her words to reach a far wider audience.

What exactly *does* happen to a girl's body sometime between the ages of ten and sixteen? Why does it happen? How is a girl to relate to these changes? And what do they mean in terms of being a Jewish woman? These are questions which all girls ask and which, throughout the ages, all mothers have tried to answer. But even the best of mothers, fortified with knowledge, love, and a good measure of common sense, might not be up to the challenge. Not everyone is adept at providing intricate physiological information, or at explaining how and why our bodies are so closely intertwined with our souls. Yet every mother will agree that all Jewish daughters deserve the most accurate and up-to-date information and the most trustworthy guidance available.

Dr. Grossman has written a book which provides all the information girls of this age require — no more and no less — together with the guidance so sorely needed. Not only does she explain, clearly and simply, the physical changes which take place in every girl's body, but also *why* they happen and what they will mean in years to come. Most important, she demonstrates in her own warm, coherent and convincing way, how these changes are part of *Hakadosh Baruch Hu*'s plan for every girl, preparing her to take her place in the long and noble line of Jewish women that began with *Sarah Imaynu* over three thousand, seven hundred years ago.

The Young Readers Division of Feldheim Publishers is proud and pleased to offer this beautiful, unique book to its readers. Written in a gentle style, but with a strong, resounding message, it presents your daughter with some of the tools she needs to become a true *bas Yisrael* and to make her way safely through today's confusing world. We are sure you will agree.

The Editor
Young Readers Division
Feldheim Publishers

Introduction

f you are a Jewish girl a year or two before bas mitzva age, this book is especially for you. As you know, reaching bas mitzva is a very important event because it means you are mature enough to know right from wrong. The Torah teaches that when you turn twelve, you start taking responsibility for your own behavior. In other words, you are on your way to becoming an adult.

Bas mitzva is not only a time when you mature in a spiritual way. This is the age (perhaps a little earlier or a little later — everybody is different) when you start to change physically too. Your body begins to develop, and by the time you finish high school, you'll look like a young woman. The thought of your body changing in this way may seem strange and even a little frightening to you now, but rest assured, it's the most normal thing in the world. Besides, who would want to look like a sixth-grader at her high school graduation?

Because it takes a while to get used to looking older, a girl of your age often feels a bit confused. She's not a little child anymore, but she's not an adult either! It's as if she's in a funny place between the two. Sometimes it's like being on a seesaw: just when you're feeling really grown-up, you get into a fight with your mother and you turn right back into a little girl again!

It's only a matter of time until you no longer feel "in between" or on a seesaw. But while it's happening, some days it may seem as if you're the only girl since Hashem created the world who has felt the way you're feeling, and you're convinced it's going to last forever!

The better you understand the changes that all girls go through, the easier it will be. I wrote this book with that in mind. As a doctor, I believe it's important for every person to be familiar with his or her body. This is especially true for girls and women, because Hashem designed our bodies to be the place where a wonderful miracle happens: the creation of a new life.

A few years ago I was asked to speak on this topic at a girls' yeshiva. It was felt that girls your age should learn about their physical development and about the importance of modesty in dress and behavior.

I was happy to accept the invitation, but then I became a little nervous. You see, when I was studying to become a doctor, we learned all about the body, but without any mention of Hashem, Who designed and created it! Unlike my professors in medical school, the girls in the yeshiva were well-versed in Torah. The challenge I faced was to present the material in a manner appropriate to my audience: girls who acknowledge the existence of Hashem, and who realize that all of creation reflects His wisdom and splendor.

But even if I succeeded in doing that, would the girls listen? Would they be interested? Would they be embarrassed? Would they ask me questions? I didn't know what to expect.

I prepared my presentation and met with girls from the sixth, seventh, and eighth grades. The students were divided into groups of ten or fifteen, and I spent one hour with each group. We spoke about development, growing up, modesty, and many other things. Their teachers were not present.

The girls were delighted that I had come to speak with them. They listened attentively and showered me with questions. (Some of the questions they asked, along with the answers I gave, are in the last chapter of this book.)

For some girls, my talk was the first they ever heard about growing up; others were already familiar with the subject. But whatever their background, everyone was interested in learning more about themselves and the ways they were changing.

Because the experience at the yeshiva was so successful, it seemed like a good idea for me to put the information into writing. That way, I would be able to reach many more girls.

That's how I came to write this book. It's a guide for Jewish girls who want to learn about growing up, but maybe aren't sure how to talk about it, or whom to ask. It explains in a clear way what happens as you mature, and why this should be a very special, exciting time in your life.

CHAPTER ONE

What You Look Like Inside

ave you ever wondered what you look like inside? When you go to the doctor and he listens to your chest and presses on your stomach, do you wonder about the sounds he hears and the shapes he feels? In this chapter we'll talk about your body and see what some of its organs look like.

Your body has a very important job. It is the home of your soul, your *neshama*. You can't see or touch your *neshama* because it is not a physical thing. The Torah teaches that the Jewish soul comes from Hashem and compares it to a spark, or a flame. Since the *neshama* comes from God, it follows that its home in this world should be a beautiful and perfect place. And so it is. The human body is an exquisite "palace" which even the most brilliant scientists, with all their sophisticated instruments, regard as a place of mystery and wonder. In fact, the more we study the human body, the more obvious it becomes how little we know about the miraculous ways in which it works.

In order to find examples of Hashem's wonderful work, we don't need an X-ray machine or a microscope. We can start with a part of us that's visible at all times: our skin. You probably don't consider your skin as important or complicated as your brain or heart. But as we're about to see, the skin has many responsibilities which it alone is capable of carrying out, responsibilities which are vital to our health.

A major function of skin is to protect the body from the outside world. For example, skin reacts to changes in temperature, and prevents the body from becoming too hot or too cold. During a warm day, your skin "knows" that by opening up its pores and releasing fluid, you'll feel cooler. This is called perspiring. On a cold day, your skin behaves differently. It saves heat. It sends some of its blood (an important source of body heat) away, into your deep organs. That's why your fingers and toes may feel very cold and lose some of their color when you're outside on a winter day. It's safer for your fingers and toes to be chilled than it is for your heart or stomach to be cold. With more blood deep inside your body and away from the cold air, these vital organs are protected, and excessive heat loss is prevented.

Our skin has another important job. It has nerve endings that give us knowledge of the world through the sense of touch. Hold this book in your hands and close your eyes. The skin on your fingers and palms will tell you that the pages are thin and smooth and have corners, and that the paper is cool and dry. How does your skin "see" so much? It has special nerves that sense these things, and they send the information to your brain. Because it is primarily with your hands that you explore the world, Hashem made the skin of your palms and fingertips rich with nerve endings.

What else does skin do? It stretches when you get bigger and it shrinks if you lose weight. It acts as a shield against bacteria and other germs that

can cause disease. When you cut yourself, your
skin knows how to close up and heal the injury.
Your skin also knows how to grow hair and nails!
And did you know that your skin can identify you
better than even your name or telephone
number? If you look closely at your fingertips,
you'll see a pattern of lines. The pattern on your
fingers is different from that of every other
person in the world!

So you see, even something as ordinary as our
skin does some very extraordinary things. When
we realize that we're talking about a part of us
that's thinner than an orange peel and lasts a
lifetime, we're even more impressed with
Hashem's handiwork. Perhaps it was this
knowledge that led King David to write:

כִּי שִׂמַּחְתַּנִי ה׳ בְּפָעֳלֶךָ בְּמַעֲשֵׂי יָדֶיךָ אֲרַנֵּן.
מַה גָּדְלוּ מַעֲשֶׂיךָ ה׳ מְאֹד עָמְקוּ מַחְשְׁבֹתֶיךָ.

תְּהִלִּים צב: ה, ו

*For You, Lord, have gladdened me with
Your deeds;
I sing for joy at the works of Your hand.
How great are Your works, O Lord;
How very profound Your thoughts!*

(Tehillim 92:5,6)

20

Now let's move underneath the skin and inside the body to explore some things we never get to see. We could talk about the stomach, the heart, or the kidneys, but because this is a book about how a girl grows up, let's look at the organs that only a girl has, and how they change as she gets older.

Hashem created a woman with a special organ whose job is to carry, protect, and feed a baby before it is born. This organ is called the uterus (YOU-ter-es) or womb (woom, rhymes with room). In Hebrew the word *rechem* – רֶחֶם or *beten* – בֶּטֶן is used. Can you think of a verse in *Sefer Bereishis* in which Hashem speaks about the uterus?

וַיִּתְרוֹצֲצוּ הַבָּנִים בְּקִרְבָּהּ...
וַיֹּאמֶר ה' לָהּ שְׁנֵי גוֹיִם בְּבִטְנֵךְ...

בְּרֵאשִׁית כה: כב, כג

And the children struggled together within her... And God said to her: Two nations are in thy womb...
(Bereishis 25:22,23)

The uterus is located a few inches below your waist between your hip bones, and it's shaped like an upside-down pear.

If you were to slice the uterus in half in order to see what's inside, this is how it would look:

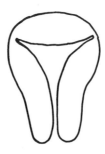

The uterus has three sides which surround an empty space called the uterine cavity. You've heard the word "cavity" before. When you get a cavity in your tooth it means there's a hole in it and you need to go to the dentist to have it filled. The cavity in the uterus is a different kind of hole. It belongs there. Hashem made this empty space so that someday a baby can grow in it. The cavity in the uterus is connected to a tube called the vagina (vah-JI-na). This tube leads down to an opening between the legs.

On each side of the uterus is a smaller structure called an ovary (OH-var-ee). Each ovary looks something like an almond, and each has a

tube — the Fallopian (fah-LOW-pee-an) tube —
connecting it with the uterine cavity.

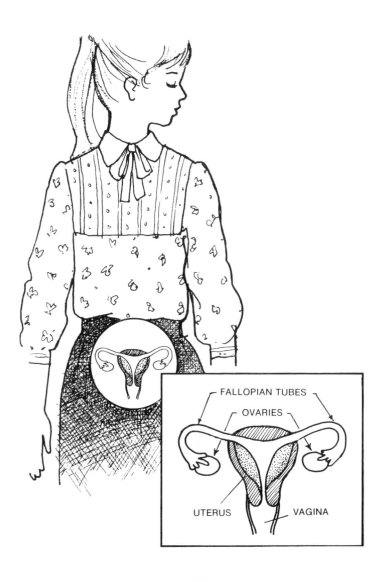

FALLOPIAN TUBES

OVARIES

UTERUS   VAGINA

The ovaries store thousands of tiny eggs. At the proper time, some of these eggs travel down the Fallopian tube to the uterine cavity, and play a role in the creation of a baby.

The uterus is an amazing organ. When it's empty, it is small, about the size of a pear, and the space inside it is tiny. When a woman is pregnant, her uterus grows bigger and bigger as the child inside her grows from a tiny seed to a full-sized baby.

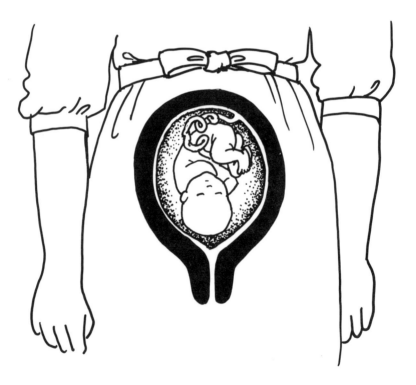

By the time a baby is ready to be born, the mother's uterus is as big as a watermelon, and the space inside it has become one thousand times larger than before she was pregnant. After the baby is born, the uterus returns to its normal size.

Look again at the picture of the baby in the uterus. Where is the opening into the vagina, on the top or the bottom? This is another interesting fact about this organ: even though the opening is on the bottom, the baby doesn't fall out. Even when there's a ten-pound baby or big twins in the uterus, it stays tightly closed and holds the babies inside until the proper time.

Another incredible thing is that the uterus knows exactly how long the baby needs to stay inside. At exactly the proper time the uterus pushes the baby out through the vagina. No scientist has been able to explain how the uterus "knows" when it's time for the baby to be born. But it does. This is one more example of the many miracles which take place in our bodies.

Let's review what we've learned about this incredible organ. It's as big as a pear, but it can grow to the size of a watermelon and then shrink back to pear-size again. For nine months it carries a baby, and even though there's an opening at the bottom, the baby doesn't fall out. The uterus knows exactly how long to hold the baby, and at the proper time, it pushes the baby out into the world.

Everyone agrees that the uterus is the perfect home for a baby before it is born. We cannot even begin to think of designing something as miraculous as a uterus. Only Hashem, Who has infinite knowledge and wisdom, could create such a wonder.

As you mature, your uterus changes and you begin to menstruate (MEN-stroo-ate). Perhaps you've never heard this word before, or you don't know what it means, but be patient. In the next chapter we will explain everything you need to know, and by the time you're finished reading, you'll be an expert on the subject!

But first, let's talk about another part of you that starts to change around bas mitzva time. We've discussed the uterus, where someday, God willing, your baby will grow. There is, however, another way you're changing, that also has to do with caring for a baby. As you mature, you begin to develop breasts. Breasts make milk for a baby after it is born.

Why did Hashem make you this way? Why can't a baby drink the same milk everyone else drinks, the kind that comes in a carton from the grocery store? What's so special about the milk from a mother's breasts? These are all good questions. As we answer them, we'll add to our list of wonders-at-work in our bodies.

Feeding a baby with breast milk is called "nursing." In Hebrew, *linok* — לִינוֹק — means "to nurse." The Hebrew word for baby — *tinok* — comes from the same root. Where in the *chumash* do we have examples of a mother nursing her child? There are several places. One is when Sarah gives birth to Yitzchak:

וַתֹּאמֶר מִי מִלֵּל לְאַבְרָהָם הֵינִיקָה בָנִים שָׂרָה כִּי יָלַדְתִּי בֵן לִזְקֻנָיו.
בְּרֵאשִׁית כא : ז

And she said, who would have suggested to Avraham that Sarah would be nursing children? For I have born him a son in his old age.

(Bereishis 21:7)

Another example is after Moshe was born and Pharaoh's daughter found him. Rashi tells us that she took Moshe and tried to have him nursed by Egyptian mothers, but he refused to drink:

שֶׁהֶחֱזִירַתּוֹ עַל מִצְרִיּוֹת הַרְבֵּה לִינַק וְלֹא יָנַק.
רַשִׁ"י, שְׁמוֹת ב : ז

28

She (Pharaoh's daughter) handed him to many Egyptian women to nurse, but he did not nurse...
(Rashi, Shemos 2:7)

Only when his sister Miriam brought their mother to feed Moshe was he happy.

Although nursing a baby is nothing new, it was only recently that scientists discovered why breast milk is the best food for an infant. Think about it. A newborn baby has never had anything to eat or drink. He's never tasted food or digested anything in his stomach. (While in the uterus, he was nourished in a different way which we'll discuss in the next chapter.) A new baby can't eat *cholent* and *kugel*. In fact, he'd probably be ill from eating simple bread and butter. His stomach isn't ready for the foods that older children eat. He must have something special. This special food is milk.

The milk that we usually buy in the grocery store is cow's milk, although some people like to drink goat's milk too. Most babies can be fed cow's milk or goat's milk, but neither are as good for them as mother's milk. This is because cow's milk is designed for newborn calves and goat's milk is made-to-order for baby goats, but the milk that best meets the needs of the newborn child is the milk that's made especially for him in his mother's breasts.

Breast milk has all the vitamins and minerals a baby needs, it is warm and sweet, and when a baby drinks it, he lies close to his mother, where it's soft and cozy. There's nothing a baby likes more than to be cradled in his mother's protective arms and to be fed this delicious food. But while he's drinking, the baby gets more than a good meal. Would you believe that a baby is protected from sickness by drinking his mother's milk? The breast milk protects him against certain viruses. It's like giving the baby his first vaccination, but without the needle!

Here's another miraculous thing about breast milk. As a baby gets older, his needs change. A baby of six months needs milk which is different from the milk a one-week-old baby needs. His mother's body "knows" this, and it adjusts the "recipe" for her breast milk according to her baby's requirements.

Some years ago, doctors tried to invent

another kind of milk which would be better for babies than breast milk. They worked for years and they tried many different formulas, but eventually they realized that mother's milk cannot be improved upon.

One of the facts scientists have discovered about nursing is that not only is it ideal for a baby, but it's also beneficial for his mother. How is breast-feeding good for a woman? Here's where we have to remember what we learned about the uterus. Hashem designed a woman so that when her baby sucks milk from her breast, a certain hormone (HOR-mone) is released in her. Hormones are chemicals that travel in the blood. They carry "messages" from one organ to another. The hormone that is released when a baby nurses travels to the uterus and tells it to shrink back to its normal size.

Now you know something about the uterus and breast-feeding. But what does all this have to do with a bas mitzva girl? It will be quite a few years before you are married and experience the blessing of giving birth to a baby. What you'd like to hear more about is the way your body is changing *now*.

CHAPTER TWO

How You're Changing

ne of the big events that happens as you grow up is called menstruation (men-stroo-AY-shun). Menstruation refers to the monthly bleeding that a girl has from her vagina. Maybe you've never heard of menstruation, or maybe you've heard it called "getting your period." Some of you have been menstruating for a while, and others haven't started yet. Whatever the case may be, you probably have many questions about this subject.

What is blood? Of course you've seen blood many times. When you scrape your knee, get a nosebleed, or cut your finger, blood comes out from the place which was hurt. We all know what blood looks like, but did you ever stop and wonder what it is, or what it does? Why is blood so important?

If you've studied biology, you've heard of the two kinds of cells in the blood: red cells and white cells. When we think of blood, we usually think of these cells. They have a significant role to play in the body, but there are many other things in the blood aside from them.

One of several vital jobs the blood performs is carrying food and water to every part of your body. Let's say you eat a slice of pizza and drink a glass of milk. What happens to the pizza and the milk after you've swallowed them? They go down to your stomach, where digestion takes place. That means that the pizza and milk are broken down into many millions of tiny, microscopic particles. If you've ever seen what happens to a sugar cube when it's dropped into a cup of hot tea, you have an idea of what happens to a piece of food in your stomach.

Once the pizza or milk is digested, the particles move into the blood vessels that are in the wall of the stomach. A blood vessel is a small pipe that carries blood to every part of your body. Even your teeth and eyes have blood vessels in them, because they need the things the blood brings them in order to stay healthy.

When you cut your finger, you've cut the smallest kind of blood vessel, called a capillary (CAP-i-ler-ee). To get an idea of how small a capillary is, take a look at one of the hairs on your head. A capillary is even skinnier than a hair! And the blood it carries is full of particles of nourishment that are smaller, *much* smaller, than the period at the end of this sentence.

What other activity is necessary to stay alive and healthy besides eating and drinking? There's something that you do all the time, even while you're sleeping. You breathe! Every few seconds, usually without thinking about it, you take some air into your lungs. Your body needs a constant supply of air in order to function. The more active you are, the more air you need. That's why, when you run up the stairs or jump rope or go swimming, you breathe faster.

Actually, it's a part of the air called oxygen (OX-i-jen) that your body needs so much. You can think of oxygen as a kind of food you can't see or taste, but which your life depends on. A person needs oxygen even more than he needs food and water. Some of you have fasted on Yom Kippur, and you probably felt hungry and weak after a few hours. But who ever heard of not breathing for that long? Being without oxygen for only three minutes puts a person's life in danger.

Luckily, it's impossible for a person to "forget" to breathe. Hashem designed our bodies to breathe automatically, and He surrounded us with precious oxygen.

What happens to the oxygen once it is in your lungs? Tiny particles of oxygen pass through the walls of the lungs into nearby blood vessels. It is the blood which brings the oxygen to every part of your body and distributes it, just as it distributes your food.

Now that we know a little about blood, let's ask another question. A baby starts out as a small seed, smaller than the seeds you find in an apple, and he grows to six, or eight, or even ten pounds by the time he's born. It takes a lot of food and oxygen to grow bones, muscles, a heart, a stomach, a brain, and all the other organs a baby has. How does this food and oxygen reach him?

Maybe some of you have already guessed the answer. A baby gets those things from his mother's blood. Just as the mother has blood vessels supplying nourishment to every part of her body, she has vessels that go to her uterus to feed the baby inside it. The blood brings food, water, vitamins, oxygen, and everything else the unborn baby needs to grow big and strong. When a pregnant woman eats a slice of pizza, the blood reaching her uterus carries some of this nourishment to the baby. When she breathes, she takes in oxygen for herself as well as for the child inside her. So you see, a mother starts taking care of her baby long before it's born.

Here's a question that might sound funny: What's a belly button? Well, a belly button is the place where every baby, before it was born, was attached to its mother. The mother and her unborn child are connected through a long cord called an umbilical (um-BIL-i-kal) cord. One end of the umbilical cord is attached to the mother's uterus, and the other end is attached to the baby. The cord looks a little like a telephone cord, because it's long and coiled. Instead of wires,

37

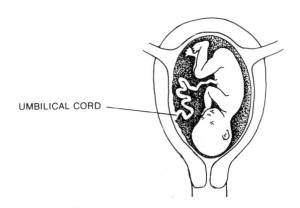

UMBILICAL CORD

an umbilical cord has blood vessels to bring
the baby all the things we've talked about.

When the baby is born, the doctor cuts the
umbilical cord. This doesn't hurt the baby or his
mother. The end of the cord which was attached
to the mother separates from the uterus and
comes out through the vagina, right after the
baby is born. Its job is done, and it can be
discarded.

Although the doctor cuts the umbilical cord
close to where it enters the baby, there is usually
a part of the cord, a little stump, left on him. This
stump falls off after a few days, and what's left in
that place is what you probably call a belly
button. It's also known as a "navel." Everyone in
the whole world has one.

Now we're experts on blood and belly buttons. What does this have to do with menstruation?

Ever since you were born, your body has been developing and learning new skills. Learning a new skill doesn't happen overnight. It takes time to practice and become comfortable doing it. Think of a baby who has just come home from the hospital. If you've ever seen a baby so young, you know how tiny and helpless he is. He is completely dependent on his mother. His abilities are limited to sleeping, eating, crying, and using up diapers.

But this stage of complete helplessness lasts only a few months. Soon the baby starts learning to lift his head, to roll over, to reach for an object. He doesn't always succeed at these new activities, but with practice he masters them. When he's a little older, he starts to crawl and then to lift himself up on his feet. But it takes some months of losing balance and falling down before he can walk by himself. The same is true of talking. A baby first uses his voice to make sounds that don't mean anything. As he gets older, he learns to turn those sounds into words, and then into sentences.

In order to someday have children, your uterus must function properly. It must be able to provide a proper "home" in which a baby can grow. When you start to menstruate, it's a sign that your body has started to practice this job.

Each month, one of the ovaries releases an egg. The egg travels through the Fallopian tube to the uterine cavity. Meanwhile, the inside lining of the uterus becomes filled with fresh blood. If pregnancy occurs, the egg begins to grow. It attaches itself to the lining of the uterus where the blood supplies the developing baby with food and oxygen. If pregnancy does not take place, the egg does not grow. Instead, the blood and the

BEFORE MENSTRUATION		MENSTRUATION	
LINING UTERUS	lining gets thicker	lining breaks down and flows slowly out of the uterus	the cycle begins again

egg flow slowly out of the body.

This whole process is called menstruation. Many girls refer to it as "getting their period," because it is the period, or the time of month, when they menstruate.

What is it like when it happens? Just as no two girls have the same nose or smile, no two girls have the same periods. Especially during the first years of menstruation, the frequency with which you get your period, as well as how much you bleed, and how long it lasts, can be different from one time to the next. No one can tell you what your periods will be like, and there's no "better" or "worse" way to menstruate. Hashem made your body so that it knows on its own what the best way is for you.

Most girls start to menstruate when they are about twelve years old, but it's normal to start any time between the age of ten and sixteen. You might get your period once, and then stop for a few months or longer before getting it again. Once your body has practiced this new activity for a while, your period will most likely come about once a month. This is what happens to most girls, but if you menstruate every three weeks or every five weeks, it's still normal.

How much blood comes out? This is a question that all girls ask. The average amount of blood that is lost during a monthly period is about six tablespoons, but the amount varies from one person to the next. One girl may bleed a lot, so that she has to change pads every few hours. (We'll talk about sanitary pads — what you wear to absorb the blood — later.) Another girl may need to change pads only two or three times a day. But it's important to know that the blood doesn't come gushing out all at once. It drips out slowly, over a number of days. It happens whether you're awake or asleep. Most girls bleed for three to five days, but some have periods as short as two days or as long as eight days. If your period is seven or eight days, the bleeding on the last days is usually very light.

Having your period can be uncomfortable. Two common complaints are breast tenderness and uterine cramps. Breast tenderness is usually felt during the days before menstrual bleeding starts. Uterine cramps feel like a stomachache, but the pain comes from the area of your uterus. They occur when the uterus contracts, squeezing blood into the vagina. Some girls never experience any menstrual cramps, and others have quite a bit of discomfort.

If you have painful cramps, here are some remedies you can try:

1. Take a warm bath and massage the area that the pain comes from.

2. Lie down with a heating pad or hot water bottle over your lower abdomen. (Check with an adult before using these things, as they can burn your skin if used incorrectly.)

3. Try one of the following exercises:
Kneel with your knees and elbows on the floor. Arch and then flex your back, the way a cat does. Breathe deeply.

Stand with your legs apart and arms at shoulder height. Twist your arms as far as you can to the left, keeping your knees straight. Then, touch your left foot with your right hand, without raising your heel from the floor. Try to reach around the outer side of your left foot and touch the heel. Do this ten times on each side, twice a day.

4. You can take some aspirin or try one of the medications that are made specifically for menstrual pain. Ask your mother or your school nurse or a doctor about them.

Occasionally, a girl has severe cramps which may keep her out of school for a few days every month. If this happens to you, you should speak to your doctor.

When you have your period, you'll wear a sanitary napkin to absorb the blood. A sanitary napkin, or pad, is made out of many layers of soft cotton. There are different sizes and styles from which to choose. Most have an adhesive strip on one side which sticks lightly to your underpants. It won't be hard for you to find a sanitary napkin that fits you and is comfortable, and you'll get used to wearing one quickly.

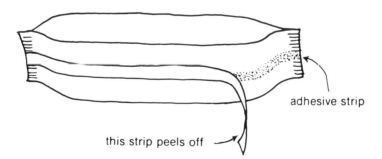

adhesive strip

this strip peels off

If you bleed heavily, you should change napkins often. Wrap the used napkin in toilet paper and throw it in the garbage. Don't put a sanitary pad in the toilet, as it can clog up the plumbing.

It's important to know the anatomy of the part of your body where your vagina is located. There are three openings in the area between your legs. These openings are completely separate from one another, just as the eyes, nose, and mouth are all separate openings on the face. The opening for urine, the urethra (yoo-REETH-ra) is close to the front of your body. It is a very small hole and you couldn't possibly put anything in it. The anus (AY-nus), the opening you use when you move your bowels, is toward the back of your body. In between these two openings is your vagina. This is where the blood leaves your body when you menstruate.

Once you begin menstruating, you'll continue getting your period for many years (except, of course, when you are pregnant and the blood is used to nourish the baby). Most women menstruate until some time in their forties. If you do some simple arithmetic, you'll discover that means you can expect to get your period approximately once a month for about thirty years. It will become a regular, expected occurrence in your life. In fact, the menstrual cycle plays a significant role in the life of a Jewish woman once she is married. There are many important *halachos* about menstruation, which you'll learn at the appropriate time.

Once a girl asked me, "I've been menstruating for a year, but my breasts are very small. Is there something wrong with me?" I told her not to worry, and explained that breast size varies a great deal from one girl to the next. It has nothing to do with menstruating or becoming a mother. Your friend may need a bra years before you, but that doesn't mean you won't both grow up and have many babies and nurse them all.

What determines when a girl will start to mature physically? There is little information about this subject. We know that each girl has an inner "clock" which regulates her physical development. One of the earliest changes in a girl's body is breast growth, and menstruation follows about two years later. Within these two years, there are other changes, such as the appearance of hair under the arms and between the legs. A girl may start to perspire in a different way, making it necessary to shower more often and to use deodorant. If you're wondering about your inner "clock," and how it's "set" to bring on these changes, it's likely that your pattern of development will follow that of your mother and older sister. But it's not certain. Everyone is different, and *your* body will change at the time that's right for *you*.

So you see, the experience of growing up is unique to each person. Think of other girls your age, and what it's been like for them. Your best friend may have started menstruating a few years ago. She's been wearing a bra for a long time, and people often think she's in high school. Maybe you just got your period for the first time this month, and had to ask your mother for help, because you weren't sure what to do. Perhaps you have a cousin or neighbor who is already fifteen, but who is still waiting for things to happen to her! There's nothing to worry about.

All three of you are perfectly normal. Be happy about how Hashem made you, and enjoy other people as they are. This, more than anything else, is a true sign of having grown up.

CHAPTER THREE

What is Modesty?

ecause we follow the laws Hashem gave us in the Torah, our lives are unlike those of other people. What are some of the activities in our lives which identify us as Jews? We observe Shabbos and *yom tov*, we follow the laws of *kashrus* and say *brachos* over our food, we pray to Hashem, we put *mezuzos* on our doors, we give *tzedaka*, ... and we dress and behave in a modest, or *tzanua* way.

It's easy to explain what keeping kosher means, or to list what is permitted or forbidden on Shabbos. But what is modesty? Can we give a simple description of what is *tznius*, and what is not? The answer is both yes, and no.

The word *tznius* — צְנִיעוּת — comes from the root *tzanoa* — צָנַע — which means "to conceal."

If we speak of *tznius* as it applies to proper dress, then we can say that, yes, there are clear guidelines for its observance in *halacha*. But a modest girl does more than cover her elbows and knees. She is *tzenua* in her thought, speech, and action as well as in her manner of dress. Modesty in this sense refers to a person's character and behavior, and would imply qualities such as humility and privacy. This aspect of *tznius* is harder to define. We'll start the discussion of modesty with what is easy to describe, and then move to what's more difficult.

The Torah has laws concerning proper dress for both men and women, but special emphasis is placed on women. Now that you are approaching bas mitzva, you have a personal obligation to begin dressing (if you haven't already done so) according to Jewish law. Remember, modest dress is required everywhere — in school and at home, as well as in camps and bungalow colonies.

Most of you are familiar with the laws and customs of modest dress.

Let's review them:

1. The neckline should be high enough to cover the collarbone, the bone at the base of the neck.
2. Sleeves should cover the elbows.
3. The hemline should be long enough to cover the knees, when sitting as well as standing.
4. In communities where it is customary for girls and women to cover their legs below the knee, *halacha* requires that this custom be carefully followed.
5. Men's or boys' clothing may not be worn by women or girls.
6. Tight blouses or skirts should not be worn.
7. Areas which are required to be covered may not be exposed even partially, such as with a slit in a skirt.

If you think about it, you'll realize that a girl who dresses according to these laws covers her body almost completely. Why does the Torah require such a high standard of modesty? We spoke in an earlier chapter about the body being a home for the soul. Let's explore this idea, and see how it leads to an answer to this question.

The Torah teaches us that man was created in two steps. First, Hashem formed him from the earth, and then He breathed life into him.

וַיִּיצֶר ה׳ אֱלֹקִים אֶת הָאָדָם עָפָר מִן הָאֲדָמָה וַיִּפַּח בְּאַפָּיו
נִשְׁמַת חַיִּים וַיְהִי הָאָדָם לְנֶפֶשׁ חַיָּה: בְּרֵאשִׁית ב: ז

And God formed man out of dust of the ground
and breathed into his nostrils the breath of life.
And man became a living creature.
(Bereishis 2:7)

The "breath of life" which God gave Adam was
his *neshama* — נְשָׁמָה — or soul. It's hard to
explain what a soul is, because you cannot see,
touch, or hear it. It cannot be weighed on a scale,
or measured with a ruler. The Torah teaches that
the Jewish soul comes from Hashem, and
compares it to a spark, or a flame. It comes
down to this world and gives life to a body. The
soul is sacred and eternal. It exists before the
body is formed and survives after the body's
death.

If you like, you may think of your soul as that
part of you which is stirred by prayer or by a
beautiful melody. It is the deepest, the innermost
essence of you.

It might sound from what you've just read that
a *neshama* is all you need to exist in this world.

Of course, that's not at all true. We live in a physical world, and Hashem has commanded us to perform physical *mitzvos*. A soul cannot give *tzedaka*, eat kosher food, or have a family. You need a body to do those things, as well as all the other commandments of the Torah.

Isn't it surprising that the soul, in order to fulfill its purpose, must be placed in a body? The soul is holy, pure, Godly; it doesn't need to eat or sleep or be vaccinated. The body gets hungry and tired, and comes down with measles and chickenpox. A soul and a body — what an unexpected match!

God created a vast number of living creatures, but only Adam was given a soul. This makes man unique in creation.

One responsibility that we have as Jews is to remind people of the holy and unique status of man. How can this be done? One way is to dress and behave in a modest manner. Dressing in a revealing way draws attention to the body, but modest dress de-emphasizes the body. It permits the attention of others to focus on our non-physical qualities, for example, on our thoughts or our personality. A girl who dresses modestly is making a significant statement. She's sending out a message which says, "My body is important, but it is only a vessel for the *real* me — my soul. I think of myself that way, and I want people to relate to me with that in mind."

The relationship of the soul to the body can be compared to that of a painting to the frame around it. A proper frame draws attention to the painting. If the frame is ostentatious, it captures the attention of the viewer, and the painting is forgotten. Similarly, if a person dresses in a revealing manner, attention is diverted from his essence — his *neshama* — to his outer "wrappings" — his body.

You have probably noticed that outside of a Torah community, there is a very different attitude about how one should dress. Wherever you are, or wherever you look — in magazines, in advertisements, in television programs, on the street — there are girls and women who dress in a revealing way. These girls are sending out the message, "I want to draw attention to my body. It's OK to be preoccupied with my figure, even though it might mean neglecting what's deep inside me." This is a sad, self-degrading way to present oneself to the world.

One word of caution: The emphasis in this chapter on the spiritual side of ourselves does not mean we are meant to disregard our physical state. To the contrary, a Jewish girl must respect her body and keep in mind the essential role it plays. The Torah instructs us to take proper care of the body and to keep it fit and free of disease. Also, having to dress modestly does not mean that one's appearance is irrelevant. We should make efforts to present ourselves in an attractive and pleasing manner. There is nothing wrong with wearing stylish clothing as long as modesty has not been sacrificed in the name of fashion.

What else identifies a modest girl besides her manner of dress? We learned that modesty means keeping concealed that which should not be revealed. How does this concept apply to the way a girl thinks and acts?

Koheles teaches us:

לַכֹּל זְמָן וְעֵת לְכָל חֵפֶץ... עֵת לַחֲשׁוֹת וְעֵת לְדַבֵּר.
קֹהֶלֶת ג: א, ז.

Everything has its season, and there is a time for every thing…a time to be silent and a time to speak… (Koheles 3:1,7)

57

A modest person knows that everything has its time and place. She knows there are times for talking and sharing feelings, and other times when her thoughts should remain her own. A *tzenua* girl understands that there are subjects which are personal, not because they are shameful or embarrassing, but because they are private and not for the whole world to know. They are for keeping in her mind and heart, and if she wishes, for sharing with someone close: her mother, sister, or friend.

This book often deals with subjects that are private. It's important for a girl to learn about the body that Hashem gave her, but she must also know that menstruation and many of the other topics covered in these pages are very personal. We don't talk about them with just anyone. On the other hand, there's nothing wrong with bringing these subjects up, in a *tzanua* way, when you're with the right person. In fact, it's a good idea to talk with someone you feel comfortable with when you're going through a new experience. You'll find that you feel much less alone and confused about what's happening if you share your thoughts with someone who's gone through it already.

You may have classmates who make jokes about menstruation and other private subjects. They giggle at one another's silly comments, and may sometimes even go so far as to insult or embarrass another girl in the class. Such behavior shows a lack of *tznius*, and whoever acts this way is guilty of both slander and embarrassing another person. The best way to deal with these girls is to ignore them. If they see there is no audience for their antics, they will soon stop them.

You will find that there are people who treat anything related to the body in a vulgar way. They write books and magazines, or make television shows and movies, using the body in a cheap, immodest fashion. In all these places, you can find the most holy of subjects treated with gross disrespect.

It is sad, but that's the way many people are, and they will probably not change until *Mashiach* comes. You, however, as a Torah Jew, must learn to discriminate in your reading, and in your choice of entertainment. To discriminate means to know the difference between proper and improper, and to make selections based on that knowledge. Keep in mind that what you read and listen to has an influence on you as a person. There is an abundance of books, magazines, records, television shows, and movies available to you. With the help of your parents and teachers, you must choose amongst them in the same way that you choose between kosher and non-kosher food.

Let's finish this chapter with an example of modesty from the Torah. In the Book of Ruth we learn that Ruth went out to the fields to gather grain in order to provide food for herself and her mother-in-law, Naomi. It was while Ruth was gathering grain that she was noticed by the owner of the field, Boaz, whom she eventually married.

What was it about Ruth that led Boaz to notice her? The Midrash states it was her modesty. Ruth was quiet and kept to herself as she worked, while other women flirted with the male harvesters. Many of the women hitched up their

skirts as they gathered grain to make it easier for
them to work, but Ruth kept hers down. Boaz
also noticed that Ruth kept herself at a distance
from the male workers, so that no one would
glance at her, while the rest of the women
gathered grain alongside the men.

Few of us will ever harvest grain in a field, but
we can all learn from Ruth's behavior. Think over
the story about Ruth, and try to find some
situation in your life where there is a choice
between modest and less than modest behavior.
How does your behavior rank? Are you more like
Ruth, or more like the other women who worked
in the field? Chances are your behavior lies
somewhere between the two extremes. Think
about it. And as you work on improving yourself
in the area of modest dress and behavior, it might
be helpful to keep in mind this *pasuk* from
Tehillim:

כָּל כְּבוּדָּה בַת מֶלֶךְ פְּנִימָה...

תְּהִלִּים מה: יד

*All the glory of the King's daughter
lies within her...*

(Tehillim 45:14)

61

CHAPTER FOUR

Let's Talk About Feelings

So far, you've learned what you look like inside, how your body changes as you mature, and what menstruation is all about. It might seem like we've covered everything there is to know about growing up. But there's another part of you — a very important part — that we haven't discussed. After all, there's more to you than just your physical body. A book about growing up wouldn't be complete without a chapter about the many different feelings a girl has when she's your age.

How do we talk about feelings? When I taught you about the uterus, I said it was as big as a pear, and I drew a diagram of its parts. But who can measure embarrassment, or draw a diagram of confusion or happiness?

Not only are emotions difficult to describe, they're always changing. You're laughing one minute and crying the next. This morning your mother seemed so kind and thoughtful, but by evening you think she's the meanest person you know. Last week you adored your best friend and shared all your secrets with her. This week you're not on speaking terms. Why do our feelings change so?

Our feelings aren't physical objects, but they are very real, and they affect the way we live and relate to others. As you get older, you'll want to start to look at your emotions and understand them. In fact, a big part of growing up is learning to control your feelings and developing sensitivity and respect towards the feelings of others.

Let's consider the various emotions that a girl may experience at this stage of her life and try to understand what they're about. Here are some comments made by sixth- and seventh-graders:

"I'm the only girl in my class to wear a bra, and everyone laughs at me."

"All my friends have been getting their period

for a long time. I wish I'd get mine already!"

For most girls, being different from their friends
causes embarrassment and concern. There is a
lot of pressure to "be like everyone else." A tall
girl might wear low heels and slouch over in an
attempt to hide her height. A short girl may feel
equally uncomfortable. She is angry and ashamed
when people think she is younger than her age,
and will do whatever she can to appear taller.
Depending on what the fashion is, a girl may
decide she is too heavy or too thin, or that she is
unhappy with her hair, her eyes, or her nose. She
may resent having to wear glasses or braces, or,
if most of her friends wear glasses or braces and
she doesn't, she may spend hours dreaming of
the day she'll get them. Whether it's her height or
her hair, how she dresses or how much she
weighs, if a girl feels different from her friends,
it can make her self-conscious and unhappy.

When a girl starts maturing physically, this
problem intensifies. Say you're spending a month
at camp. Most of the girls in your bunk were
together last summer, and you had a great time.
But this year things are very different. All of a

sudden, the girls in your bunk are only interested in who has started wearing a bra or menstruating. If you have matured earlier than the others, or if all the girls have changed dramatically since last summer and you haven't, your experience in camp this year may have some very unhappy moments.

What can a girl do when she's feeling unhappy because she looks too grown up, or not grown up enough?

Let's begin by talking about the desire to "be like everyone else." Is it really something to strive for? If everyone had the same features and the same personality, would the world be a better place? Imagine a party with your friends. Would it be more fun if you were all identical to one another, with the same interests and talents, and the same sense of humor?

Of course not. Life would be pretty boring if everyone looked and acted the same way. People are not like cookies made with a cookie cutter. One of the miracles of creation is that each of us is unique. There has never been, and there never will be, another girl who looks, thinks, and feels exactly like you. You were born to look and think and feel like YOU, not like someone else. That's the way Hashem created the world.

What about someone who makes embarrassing remarks about another girl's development? We talked about this in the previous chapter. Only an immature girl who is lacking in *tznius* acts this way. Furthermore, the Torah clearly prohibits any behavior that is meant to shame another person.

Here is another comment, made by a girl about twelve years old:

"I'm so afraid of getting my period. It could happen any day. What if I'm not prepared?"

Most girls are anxious about what will happen the first time they menstruate. They imagine all sorts of embarrassing scenes in which they are caught unprepared when they get their period for the first time.

The first time you menstruate, you probably won't even be aware of it until you go to the toilet and notice some blood on your underpants, or on the toilet paper. Most girls bleed very little when they start menstruating. If you don't have a pad, use some tissues instead. They will absorb any blood that drips out. Don't worry about bleeding so much that it stains your clothing. That much bleeding just doesn't happen when you are starting your period.

What about your feelings? How will you feel about beginning to menstruate? Again, everyone is different. Your reaction will depend a great deal upon how well you understand what menstruation is, and upon what impressions you have about it from your mother, sisters, and friends. A girl who has never heard of menstruation and one day finds herself bleeding from her vagina, will be frightened and worried. Someone who has been led to believe that menstruation is a sickness or makes her dirty will also have negative feelings about it.

One reason I wrote this book was to teach girls like you that menstruation is a normal, natural function of their bodies. There is no reason for fear or worry when you get your period. It means your body is doing exactly what it is supposed to do.

Once you start menstruating regularly, you may notice that you tend to feel a particular way during the days you have your period, or just before it comes. I asked girls how they feel around the time they menstruate, and here's what they said:

"I get very moody. I'm more sensitive, and I cry easily."

"I like to be active, so I take a lot of walks, and I exercise."

"I like to be alone. The first day of my period, I usually read, or take a nap."

"I invite a lot of friends over, and we bake cakes and cookies."

"I'm not any different during my period than I am the rest of the month. I usually forget that I have it."

Sometimes a girl asks me why her body begins to menstruate now, if she isn't going to have a baby until she's much older? Why doesn't it just start when she gets married? Why do you have to "practice" menstruating? It's a good question. What do you think the answer is?

Certainly Hashem made us this way for a reason. Maybe He felt that bas mitzva is a good time to remind a girl that she is not going to stay a child forever. Someday she'll have the responsibilities of marriage and motherhood, and what she makes of herself now will determine what kind of wife and mother she'll become. This is what one fifteen-year-old girl answered when I asked what her thoughts are when she menstruates:

When I get my period, it makes me stop and think about the day when, God willing, I'll be a mother. I know that menstruating means that my body knows how to prepare for having a baby grow in it. I like to imagine what it will be like to be a mother, and I think about what kind of person I hope to be by then. It makes me consider seriously who I am now, and what I'm doing to improve myself. So even though my period sometimes makes me a little uncomfortable, when I get it I feel happy inside. I'm proud to be growing up.

CHAPTER FIVE

Some Questions and Answers from a Talk with Twelve-Year-Olds

71

SARA: What if I get my period for the first time in the middle of a class?

DR. G: For most girls, the first period involves very light bleeding. Usually it's hardly more than enough to stain your underpants. Chances are, you won't know you are menstruating until you get undressed or go to the toilet.

If it does happen that you feel you are getting your period and you're in the middle of a class, you can excuse yourself and go to the restroom. Some restrooms have machines from which you can buy a napkin. If there is no machine, or you don't have any money, you can go to the office or the school nurse and ask for a sanitary napkin. There's no reason to be embarrassed. Every grown woman has been menstruating for years and will be glad to help you. It's very rare to bleed so much that it stains your clothing, but if it happens, you can ask permission to go home to change.

RIVKA: I'm twelve and my cousin is eleven. Why has she started menstruating and I haven't?

DR. G: I'm sure that there are many other ways

that you and your cousin differ aside from this
one. As we've said, it's normal for a girl to start
her periods at any time between the ages of ten
and sixteen. When she starts has nothing to do
with her ability to have children later on. There is
nothing for you to worry about. Hashem created
you in such a way that your body knows the
perfect time for you to start menstruating.

DINA: How come I sometimes get moody and I
don't feel like talking to anyone? It never used to
happen when I was younger.
DR. G: The hormones that travel around your
body, causing you to grow taller, develop breasts,
and menstruate, also have an effect on your
emotions. There may be times when you are
more sensitive, and easily angered or hurt. This
happens to some girls around the time they have
their period, but you may notice it at other times
of the month as well. The years during which a
girl or boy grows up are full of new experiences
and emotions. There are wonderful moments, but
there may be difficult ones also. Perhaps there
are days when you feel confused about things

and you get into arguments with people, especially members of your family. You may want to spend some time by yourself, to think about things. There's nothing wrong with this. Being alone for a while may help you gather your thoughts and see things in a fresh perspective.

NAOMI: Why does my skin break out around the time of my period?

DR. G: The skin on your face has many tiny oil glands. Each gland has a pore, or opening, which normally is so small that you can't see it. When you menstruate, there are high levels of a hormone that causes the oil glands to be more active. If a pore gets clogged up, then the oil can't get out, and you get a pimple. Pimples are very common during the years when you mature. What can you do to prevent pimples? Keep your face and hair clean, and watch what you eat. Some people find that avoiding certain foods, such as chocolate, nuts, and fried foods, helps keep their skin clear. There are also some medications you can buy in a drugstore to treat your skin if it breaks out in pimples. If you feel you have a very difficult problem with your skin and nothing you do seems to help, you may want to see a dermatologist, a doctor who specializes in skin problems.

ESTHER: Can I tell my father when I start menstruating?
DR. G: If you feel comfortable telling him, there's no reason why you can't, as long as it's done in a personal, private way.

LEAH: When I have my period, will I have trouble going to the toilet?
DR. G: No. When you menstruate, the blood comes out of your vagina. The vagina is an opening which is different from the openings you use to urinate or have a bowel movement. There is no connection between them.

DEVORA: How active can I be when I have my period?
DR. G: This depends entirely on how you feel. There is no reason to refrain from any activity, if you feel up to it. In fact, some girls say that being

active and busy makes their cramps go away. Of course, if you are wearing a sanitary pad, you can't go swimming.

RIVKA: Isn't it harmful for me to lose blood every month? Doesn't my body need this blood?
DR. G.: Compared to the total amount of blood in your body, the amount that you lose during your period is very small. There are cells in the middle of some of your bones whose job is to make new blood cells. They easily replace the blood you lose during menstruation.

ESTHER: When should a girl start wearing a bra?
DR. G.: Your body matures over time. At first, you'll probably be the only person to know that your breasts have started to develop. After a while, you will have changed enough so that it is obvious to other people. At this point, you will probably start wearing a bra.

RACHEL: Why do people giggle and make silly jokes about these things?
DR. G.: Children often think that things related to how the body works are funny. As you mature, you'll find these jokes less and less amusing.

Conclusion

Well, here we are at the end of the book. I hope you've learned many new things about growing up and changing, and that you've found them interesting and challenging. I've tried to answer all the questions you might have about becoming a young woman, but I'm sure I've forgotten a few. If you've read this book carefully and still have questions, or if you are confused about something, you should ask an older girl or woman about it.

If there isn't anyone around that you feel comfortable talking with, feel free to write me. In fact, I'd like to hear from you even if you don't have a question. Did you like this book? Do you have any suggestions on how it could be improved? Please share your comments and ideas with me.

Miriam Grossman, MD

c/o Feldheim Publishers

200 Airport Executive Park

Spring Valley, NY 10977

Have fun growing up, and mazal tov on your bas mitzva!

I would like to thank the following people for their
encouragement and assistance:
Mrs. Leah Klein, Mrs. Bronya Shaeffer
and Prof. H. Branover.

Glossary of Hebrew and Yiddish words

(Y = Yiddish); (pl. = plural); (f. = feminine)

BAS MITZVA: a Jewish girl at age twelve, now responsible for keeping all the commandments.

BEREISHIS: Genesis, the first book of the Bible.

BRACHOS: blessings.

CHOLENT (Y): a Sabbath food, usually made from potatoes, beans or rice, and meat, cooked on Friday and left on the fire until Saturday morning.

CHUMASH: the Five Books of Moses, or one of the Five Books.

HALACHA, HALACHOS (pl.): Torah law.

HASHEM: God.

KASHRUS: keeping kosher.

KOHELES: the Book of Ecclesiastes in the Bible, written by King Solomon.

KUGEL (Y): a baked food, usually made of noodles, rice or potatoes.

LINOK: to nurse.

MASHIACH: the Messiah.

MAZAL TOV: "congratulations."

MEZUZA, MEZUZOS (pl.): a handwritten parchment placed on the doorposts in Jewish homes.